RSL 8+ to 10+ Comprehensic

These papers are accompanied by detailed, *teaching* mark schemes, designed to communicate the most important exam skills to students of all abilities. Unlike in **RSL 11+ Comprehension**, all the papers are structured similarly, with 25 marks available for each one: while the tests increase in difficulty throughout the book, this consistent format should help students to feel comfortable while they learn.

At the same time, the papers are designed to be challenging. Children who have worked through them all should be well prepared for most comprehension exams up to 10+ level.

The solution pages not only mark, but thoroughly teach the lessons from each exercise (all things that I say frequently to my students). The explanations have not been designed for a student of this age to use independently: they have been created with a supportive adult in mind. This book allows any parent to step confidently into the role of a tutor.

Please bear in mind that the example solutions are *no more than suggestions*. Very few of them claim to be the only possible approach. Read the discussion around each one if you want advice for assessing a different answer.

Although these papers have been carefully crafted in response to the exams set by many schools in recent years, they cannot imitate every design of test. However, the skills of reading and analysis addressed in this book will be a valuable preparation for any type of comprehension.

If, having completed this book, you're interested in helping your child develop their skills further, you may be interested in reading about my *11 Plus Lifeline* service. Visit **www.11pluslifeline.com** to learn more.

How To Use This Book: Advice For Students

These materials can be used in different ways. For example, you may wish to answer some papers while reading the solutions, in order to understand how a comprehension exam works. However, most people will choose to write their answers then refer to the marking sheet.

When you are correcting your work, it is a good idea to take notes of any important points: this will help you to remember them. If your answer could be improved, it is often worth re-writing it with reference to the mark scheme.

These papers will be most useful if you complete them in order. Although each test and mark sheet can stand alone, used in sequence they will build up your skills steadily.

The papers in this book have been designed for use without time limits, because they are focused on teaching each student to produce skilful, carefully written answers. When these skills have been acquired, it is usually a fairly simple matter to speed them up with the past papers available from many schools. Timing problems are almost always caused by a lack of confidence with core techniques. Having said this, if you wish to complete a paper in timed conditions, 30-40 minutes will generally present an appropriate level of challenge.

Essential Advice For Comprehension Tests

- ✓ Read the passage; underline anything you do not fully understand.
- ✓ Read the questions.
- ✓ Return to your underlined phrases and work them out as best you can, now that you know the full context.
- ✓ Underline the key words in each question as you come to it (e.g. "why", "own words", "evidence", "lines 20-23").
- ✓ Look at the number of marks available for the question, and work out how your answer should be structured.
- ✓ Read the necessary paragraph(s) and underline any useful evidence. Keep underlining and quotations short, if possible (usually no more than six words).
- ✓ After writing your answer, check that you have answered every part of the question and have written enough for the number of marks.
- ✓ Check your English, and move on to the next question.

Never leave a blank space! If all else fails, make an educated guess. You might still get marks.

Finally, never cross out an answer unless you have already *completed* an improved one.

Also Available

11 Plus Lifeline (printable resources for all 11+ subjects): **www.11pluslifeline.com**

RSL Creative Writing (several volumes)

RSL 11+ Comprehension: Books 1 & 2
RSL 11+ Comprehension, Multiple Choice: Books 1 & 2
RSL 11+ Maths
RSL 13+ Comprehension

GCSE Maths by RSL, Higher Level (9-1), Non-Calculator
GCSE Spanish by RSL
GCSE French by RSL
GCSE German by RSL

Contents

I recommend **cutting out the comprehension passages along the dotted lines**, so that they are always in view while answering the questions. This will encourage students to refer back to the text on every possible occasion and to write focused, properly evidenced answers.

RSL 8+ to 10+ Comprehension

RSL 8+ to 10+ Comprehension (3rd edition)

by Robert Lomax

Published by RSL Educational Ltd

Copyright © RSL Educational Ltd 2021

Company 10793232

VAT 252515326

Registered in England & Wales

Cover design by Heather Macpherson at Raspberry Creative Type

Image on 11 Plus Lifeline information page © iStockPhoto.com.

Cover images & graphics © Shutterstock.com.

www.rsleducational.co.uk

We are a family business in a competitive marketplace. We want to improve and expand our range, providing even better products for our customers, including families who may not wish to purchase long courses of private tuition. If you have any feedback, please let me know! My email address is **robert@rsleducational.co.uk**.

If you like this book, please tell your friends and write a review on Amazon!

1. What job do Shiro's owners do? **(1)**

……………………………………………………………………………………………………

2. The good old couple are only sad about one thing.

(a) What is it? **(1)**

……………………………………………………………………………………………………

(b) Explain how this affects their feelings for Shiro. **(1)**

……………………………………………………………………………………………………

……………………………………………………………………………………………………

3. Write down two facts about Shiro's appearance. **(2)**

(i) ……………………………………………………………………………………………

(ii) ……………………………………………………………………………………………

4. What does the old man eat for his supper? **(1)**

……………………………………………………………………………………………………

5. Explain why "the happiest hour of the day both for the old man and his dog" (lines 14-15) is when the man finishes his supper. **(2)**

……………………………………………………………………………………………………

……………………………………………………………………………………………………

6. What do you think "frugal" means (line 16)? Explain how the ideas in the passage support your answer. **(2)**

……………………………………………………………………………………………………

……………………………………………………………………………………………………

……………………………………………………………………………………………………

7.   Using your own words as far as possible, explain how we know that the
      neighbours are "wicked and cruel" (line 22).   **(3)**

....

....

....

....

8.   Explain why the old man thinks that birds are "attacking the corn" (line 26).

                                                                            (1)

....

....

9.   Explain what is meant by:

      (a) industriously (line 29)   **(1)**

....

      (b) bewilderment (line 31)   **(1)**

....

10.   Who is stronger, Shiro or his master? Explain your answer, using evidence from
      the final paragraph.   **(2)**

....

....

....

11.   From the passage, write down:

      (a) an adjective   ....   **(1)**

      (b) an adverb   ....   **(1)**

12. Taking some ideas from the picture, write the next paragraph of the story. Be as creative as you can, and be careful with your spelling and grammar. **(5)**

....

....

....

....

....

....

....

....

....

....

....

....

TOTAL 25

Shiro – *Solutions*

Most of the questions ask for facts or simple explanations; the challenge is to find the information in the text and present it clearly. Question 7 is a little trickier, and Question 11 expects you to know some parts of speech.

---

1. **What job do Shiro's owners do?**	**(1)**
They are farmers.	

Any answer based on "farming a small plot of land" is fine here.

A common mistake in this comprehension is to confuse Shiro's owners with the "wicked and cruel" neighbours, because both couples are referred to as an "old man and his wife".

- It's a good idea to **underline the places where people are mentioned** when you read a comprehension text, and carefully work out who is who. This way you will avoid mixing up characters and losing marks.

Notice how it's possible to write a full sentence answer without using lots of words!

Marking: Anything to do with being farmers or working on a plot of land.   **[1 mark]**

---

2. **The good old couple are only sad about one thing.**	
(a) What is it?	**(1)**
It is that they have "no child".	

This is slightly trickier than Question 1, because the text uses the phrase "apart for one great sorrow": if you only look through the passage for the word "sad", you won't find the answer.

However, it's worth bearing in mind that the **early questions** in a comprehension are likely (though not certain) **to focus on the beginning of the passage**. This way you can narrow your search: only look further if you are unable to find the right answer in the first few lines.

Another clue is that the question mentions "**one** thing", and the passage refers to "**one** great sorrow": even without knowing the word "sorrow", you might be able to guess the answer this way.

Marking: Correct answer only, with a quote or in own words.   **[1 mark]**

> ### (b) Explain how this affects their feelings for Shiro. (1)
>
> This means that they love Shiro more, to make up for not having a child.

This is the first genuinely challenging question in the paper, because it requires you to work out an idea that is not actually stated in the text.

Also, the language in the phrase "on him they lavished all the affection of their old age" is difficult.

However, there are a few ways through these difficulties:

- If you know the word "affection", try not to be distracted by "lavished": it is possible to work out the meaning of the sentence without it.

- Always **read on for clues**: the next sentence says that the couple "loved [Shiro] so much" that they gave him their own food.

- The section talking about the old people's love for Shiro comes directly after the sentence that says they did not have a child.

Your challenge is to draw a sensible connection between the ideas in the text.

The second part of the example answer ("to make up for not having a child") makes things clear, but probably isn't necessary in this 1-mark question.

> **Marking:** Needs to say that it makes them love Shiro more. **[1 mark]**

> ### 3. Write down two facts about Shiro's appearance. (2)
>
> **(i)** He is white.
>
> **(ii)** He looks like a small wolf.

It wouldn't be relevant to write that he is a "real Japanese dog": in itself, this doesn't tell you anything about how he looks.

Any point that could apply to *any* dog would not get a mark: for example, saying that he "has paws" wouldn't tell us anything about Shiro *in particular*. Neither would anything that is not to do with appearance: for example, that he "barks".

> **Marking:** Any points clearly about Shiro's individual appearance and based on the text. **[2 marks]**

> **4.**   **What does the old man eat for his supper?**   **(1)**
>
>   He eats "rice and vegetables".

You need to mention both of these things for the mark. One or the other should receive a half mark.

> **Marking:** 0.5 marks each for "rice" and "vegetables".   **[1 mark]**

> **5.**   **Explain why "the happiest hour of the day both for the old man and his dog" (lines 14-15) is when the man finishes his supper.**   **(2)**
>
> This is when the man feeds bits of his food to Shiro. Shiro likes to eat, and the old man is happy to be kind to him.

You need to re-read the whole of the second paragraph to understand this fully.

To be certain of both marks, you should explain:

- why the man is happy;
- why Shiro is happy.

This is because the question quotes the phrase "the old man and his dog". They aren't happy for exactly the same reason, so you need to explain both.

> **Marking:** 1 mark for a simple explanation of why the man is happy. 1 mark for why Shiro is happy.   **[2 marks]**

> **6.**   **What do you think "frugal" means (line 16)? Explain how the ideas in the passage support your answer.**   **(2)**

This question needs a reasonably accurate **definition** of "frugal", and a sensible **explanation** of how the passage backs this up:

> "Frugal" means "simple", because the old man only eats "rice and vegetables".

Here is another good way to answer the question:

> A "frugal" meal is a small one, because the old couple must "deny themselves" to feed Shiro, which means that they don't have much food.

Even if you already know what "frugal" means, the question requires you **to explain it**, based on the passage.

> **Marking:** 1 mark for the meaning, 1 mark for a connected example from the passage. If not completely clear how the example supports the definition, award 1.5. **[2 marks]**

> **7.** **Using your own words as far as possible, explain how we know that the neighbours are "wicked and cruel" (line 22).** **(3)**
>
> They dislike the good couple and Shiro. They attack Shiro, even hurling things at him, when he comes to their house. Sometimes they hurt him very badly.

"Using your own words" means that you need to give **all the most important information** that answers the question, but **without copying the wording of the passage**. This way, you will show that you fully understand what the passage means.

The process for answering a question of this sort is quite simple.

(Don't worry: you will have many chances to practise it as you work through this book!)

 ✓ **Identify and underline each idea in the text:**

Next door to this good old couple there lived another old man and his wife who were both wicked and cruel, and who <u>hated their good neighbours and the dog Shiro</u> with all their might. Whenever Shiro <u>happened to look into their kitchen</u> they at once <u>kicked him</u> or <u>threw something at him</u>, sometimes even <u>wounding him</u>.

 ✓ **Translate each idea into your own words:**

hated their good neighbours and the dog Shiro	dislike the good couple and Shiro
happened to look into their kitchen	comes to their house
kicked him	attack Shiro
threw something at him	even hurling things at him
wounding him	they hurt him very badly

Notice that I have moved everything into the present tense. You don't have to do this – see my discussion of **Question 8**.

 ✓ **Now link the ideas together in a way that makes sense:**

> They <u>dislike the good couple and Shiro</u>. They <u>attack Shiro</u>, <u>even hurling things at him</u>, when he <u>comes to their house</u>. Sometimes <u>they hurt him very badly</u>.

The following answer would not get any marks, because it **repeats information that has already been given in the question**, and because **it does not use "your own words"**:

> *We know that they are like this because the passage calls them "wicked and cruel".*

Marking: See above. An answer including all the main ideas, but not written in own words, would be worth 2. So would an answer in own words but with things missing. If more is wrong with the answer, it might still get 1 mark for some relevant content.
[3 marks]

8.	**Explain why the old man thinks that birds are "attacking the corn" (line 26).**
(1)

He thinks this because Shiro is barking in the field.

It's usual to **write an answer in the present tense when the question is also written this way**.

However, it is also acceptable to write in the past tense, **so long as you are consistent within each answer**:

He thought this because Shiro was barking in the field.

Compare the following answer. Can you see what is wrong with it (although it would probably get the mark)?

He thinks this because Shiro was barking in the field.

Obviously, it would be weird to write in any tense apart from the past or present:

He will think this because Shiro will be barking in the field.

That *might* still get the mark, but it is more than slightly peculiar!

Marking: Correct answer only.					**[1 mark]**

9.	**Explain what is meant by:**

	(a) industriously (line 29)					**(1)**

This means that Shiro is working hard.

Any answer that says Shiro is digging determinedly, quickly, or with concentration should get a mark here.

You could also just write:

It means "working hard".

… or:

It means "determinedly".

Any similar answer should be fine. You don't have to use quotation marks.

✓ Although you may not know the word "industriously", you should be able to come close to its meaning by **covering it** and asking yourself **which other words might make sense in the same place**:

- "slowly"?
- "carefully"?
- "quickly"?

The next step is to choose the best one of the possibilities you've found. It is unlikely that a dog would dig slowly or carefully while "yelping with joy", so "quickly" is the best of these three options. It isn't *exactly* right, but it would get the mark.

> **Marking:** Any of the correct examples above, or something similar to them. A vaguely reasonable but incorrect guess should get 0.5 marks. **[1 mark]**

> **(b) bewilderment (line 31)** (1)
>
> This means "confusion".

The clue for this comes from "unable to understand what it all meant", earlier in the same sentence.

> **Marking:** As for **(a)**. **[1 mark]**

> **10. Who is stronger, Shiro or his master? Explain your answer, using evidence from the final paragraph.** (2)
>
> Shiro is stronger, because he can "drag" his master by his clothes.

It is not possible to say with *certainty* that Shiro is stronger: perhaps his master would be able to drag him if the situation were reversed.

However, this is the most reasonable possible answer, based on the information in the final paragraph.

Another sensible answer, such as that Shiro is digging "with all his might" while his master "looks on", would also be fine. (However, there are more likely explanations for this than Shiro being stronger: he is better at digging – but more importantly, he is the one who thinks he is going to find something!)

> **Marking:** 1 mark for Shiro, 1 mark for a sensible reason based on the final paragraph. **[2 marks]**

---

11.   From the passage, write down

(a) an adjective   (1)

small

An **adjective** describes a **noun** ("the kitchen is **small**"; "a **wrinkly** elephant").

Marking: Any adjective from the text.   [1 mark]

(b) an adverb   (1)

industriously

An **adverb** describes a **verb**: in other words, it explains **the way in which a thing is done**.

- Very often, an adverb will end with "-ly" ("She chewed the crisps angrily." "Thoughtfully, Andrew drew a helicopter in the margin of his comprehension paper").

To start with, you need to be able to recognise **nouns**, **adjectives**, **verbs** and **adverbs**. Other parts of speech (such as pronouns and prepositions) are less vital and can come later!

Marking: Any adverb from the text.   [1 mark]

---

12.   Taking some ideas from the picture, write the next paragraph of the story. Be as creative as you can, and be careful with your spelling and grammar.   (5)

All of a sudden, Shiro yelped and pulled back, licking his paw sheepishly. The old man knelt beside the hole, the smell of fresh earth in his nose. Something hard was poking through the soil. It had a cool, smooth surface, which flickered in the early morning light. Taking a tool from by the fence, the man slowly prised into view a little silver box. As he patted the dust from its lid, it made a hollow, dull sound. Shiro, who had forgotten his bruised paw, was staring. Neither of them noticed their neighbour's face, twisted with glee, peering through the parted corn.

Your answer needs to **carry on effectively from where the passage ends**, sounding as though it is part of the same tale. **<u>You do not need to finish the story</u>**.

The example is quite simple: it is written in short sentences, but these are varied so that they begin in different ways.

Notice how it uses the following senses:

sight	"flickered in the early morning light"
hearing	"a hollow, dull sound"
smell	"smell of fresh earth"
touch	"cool, smooth surface"

Only taste is missing, out of the most common list of five senses.

There are **adverbs** like "sheepishly" and **adjectives** such as "hollow". However, an even more important feature is the use of **interesting verbs** such as "yelped", "flickered" and "prised". These make the actions in the story seem interesting.

- Imagine how much less engaging my answer would have been if, instead of these three verbs, I had written "barked", "shone" and "pulled". These verbs are much less specific. They make it harder to imagine what is happening clearly.

Finally, because the question asks you to "take ideas from the picture", the example refers to the **tool** (perhaps a spade or a hoe) in the image, to **the master taking over**, and to **the person peering through the plants** in the background.

Marking: A 5-mark answer will follow on directly from where the story finishes and will include some extra information that is in the picture but not the text. The characters will clearly be the same people as in the passage: they won't have changed their personalities. It will use at least two thirds of the answer space, and will include a wide variety of interesting language. It will have very few English errors: if there are any, they will be minor. Use your judgement to subtract marks if elements of the above are missing. Marks below 3 should only be awarded if an answer is very weak.

[5 marks]

END

Blank Page

Paper 2: *The Lamplighter*

This paper focuses on teaching you to explain simple ideas clearly. As in the previous paper, 'Shiro', there's also the chance to practise writing answers in your own words.

Robert Louis Stevenson was a Scottish author, famous for books including 'Treasure Island' and 'Strange Case of Dr Jekyll and Mr Hyde'.

My tea is nearly ready and the sun has left the sky;
It's time to take the window to see Leerie going by;
For every night at teatime and before you take your seat,
With lantern and with ladder he comes posting up the street.

5   Now Tom would be a driver and Maria go to sea,
And my papa's a banker and as rich as he can be;
But I, when I am stronger and can choose what I'm to do,
O Leerie, I'll go round at night and light the lamps with you!

For we are very lucky, with a lamp before the door,
10   And Leerie stops to light it as he lights so many more;
And O, before you hurry by with ladder and with light,
O Leerie, see a little child and nod to him to-night!

      By Robert Louis Stevenson

Blank Page

1.   **(a)** What is the lamplighter called?   **(1)**

....

      (b) When does he work?   **(2)**

....

....

      (c) Fully explain what he has to do and why it needs to be done.   **(2)**

....

....

....

2.   Where is the narrator (the boy) when he watches the lamplighter?   **(1)**

....

3.   Re-write lines 5-6 in your own words.   **(4)**

....

....

....

....

4.   Write down two words from the text that rhyme with each other.   **(1)**

....

5.   How quickly does the lamplighter work? Which word from lines 9-12 tells you
        this?   **(2)**

....

....

6.   Explain why the narrator is "lucky".   **(2)**

....

....

....

7.   Does the narrator want to be "rich" like his father? Explain your answer.   **(2)**

....

....

....

8.   **(a)** List two details from the picture that you do not find in the passage.   **(2)**

....

....

        (b) List two details from the passage that you do not find in the picture.   **(2)**

....

....

9. Would you have liked to be a lamplighter? Using details from the passage or the picture (or both), explain your answer. **(4)**

....

....

....

....

....

....

....

....

TOTAL 25

The Lamplighter – *Solutions*

The main challenge here is to get into the boy's mind, and understand how excited he is about the lamplighter's daily routine. Otherwise, questions such as 6 and 7 will be difficult.

---

1. (a) What is the lamplighter called?	**(1)**
He is called Leerie.	

Comprehensions often begin quite simply like this, to give you some confidence. Don't assume that later questions will be as easy, and lose concentration!

Notice how it is possible to give a full sentence answer without writing "The lamplighter is called Leerie," by using a **pronoun**: "he".

Marking: Needs to mention "Leerie". Even a one-word answer is fine here.   **[1 mark]**

(b) When does he work?	**(2)**
He works every night, soon after sunset.	

If your answer mentions sunset, dusk, or evening, you are likely to get 2 marks. You will get 1 mark for a less specific answer – that he works "at night", for example.

✓ The lesson here is that you need to **keep an eye on the number of marks available**. When there are 2 marks for what may seem like a 1-mark question, it's a clue that extra care is needed.

Marking: See discussion above.   **[2 marks]**

(c) Fully explain what he has to do and why it needs to be done.	**(2)**
Leerie walks through the town, lighting the lamps. This will keep the streets bright at night.	

When you have a question that asks more than one thing, **underline each part of the question** so that you can easily check that you have done everything – like this:

<u>Fully</u> <u>explain</u> <u>what</u> he has to do and <u>why</u> it needs to be done.   <u>(2)</u>

Have you discussed "**what** he has to do"? Have you "explained" "**why**" he must do it? Have you explained both points "**fully**": so that they are completely clear? Does your answer offer at least **two** things for the marker to tick?

There are various things you could write for the "why" part of the question, because this isn't made fully clear in the poem. For instance, you could say that it is to stop people having accidents in the dark, or to discourage criminals.

> **Marking:** 2 marks for a clear explanation of what and why. 1 mark if unclear or if something important is missing. **[2 marks]**

> **2.** **Where is the narrator (the boy) when he watches the lamplighter?** **(1)**
>
> He is standing inside the window.

This might be confusing, because the text says that it is "time to take the window", which is an old-fashioned way of putting things. However, you should be able to build a sensible answer from the word "window".

 ✓ A reasonable and close answer such as *He is leaning out of the window*, though not necessarily correct, should also get the mark.

However, *He is at home* or *He is in the place where he eats his tea* would get half a mark at best. These answers are too vague to be worth more.

> **Marking:** Any answer that describes him being at the window, just inside it, or looking out of it. **[1 mark]**

> **3.** **Re-write lines 5-6 in your own words.** **(4)**
>
> Tom wants to become a driver and Maria wants to be a sailor, and my dad is very rich because he works in a bank.

Remember the system from your previous paper:

 ✓ **Identify and underline each idea from the text:**

Now <u>Tom would be a driver</u> and <u>Maria go to sea</u>,
And <u>my papa's a banker</u> and <u>as rich as he can be</u>;

 ✓ **Translate each idea into your own words:**

Tom would be a driver	Tom wants to become a driver
Maria [would] go to sea	Maria wants to be a sailor
my papa's a banker	my dad works in a bank
as rich as he can be	very rich

(Once you're comfortable with this method, you will be able to skip the step of writing out a translation for each idea. You will be able to do it in your head, or take quick notes.)

✓ **Link the ideas together in a way that makes sense:**

> <u>Tom wants to become a driver</u> and <u>Maria wants to be a sailor</u>, and <u>my dad</u> is <u>very rich</u> because he <u>works in a bank</u>.

Sometimes you will need to chop your ideas up and move them around a bit, as I have done here, in order to create a clear and simple sentence.

> **Marking:** 4 marks for a clearly written answer, consistently in own words, which contains all the ideas set out above. Subtract marks for missing elements or significant amounts of word-borrowing from the passage.   **[4 marks]**

> 4.   **Write down two words from the text that rhyme with each other.**   **(1)**
>
> "sky"   "by"

Any pair of rhyming words is fine here. The question is testing that you understand what **rhyme** is.

✓ Words **rhyme** when they **end with the same sound, or a very similar sound**. "Fine" and "line" rhyme, but "fine" and "lime" do not.

"Write down" means that you do not have to use a full sentence here.

> **Marking:** Any pair of rhyming words from the poem. They do not have to be near each other or at the ends of lines.   **[1 mark]**

> 5.   **How quickly does the lamplighter work? Which word from lines 9-12 tells you this?**   **(2)**
>
> He is a fast worker. I know this because of the word "hurry".

Be careful in a question like this that you **answer both parts** – even though they are similar.

✓ This is why you should **underline the important words in a question** before answering it.

It is also wise, when a question says something like "from lines 9-12", to **put brackets or a box around that section of the passage**. This way you won't accidentally write about other parts of the text!

Marking: 1 mark for "quickly", "fast", "rapidly" or similar. 1 mark for "hurry".

[2 marks]

---

6.   **Explain why the narrator is "lucky".**   (2)

He is lucky to have a lamp "before" his door, so he can get a good view when Leerie lights it.

For 2 marks, you need to recognise that the lamp is outside the door of the house, and you need to explain why this makes the narrator "lucky".

The second part isn't clear, so you could also write something like this:

He is lucky to have a lamp "before" his door, so the area outside his house is well lit and safe.

Any sensible reason is fine.

Marking: See discussion above.   [2 marks]

---

7.   **Does the narrator want to be "rich" like his father? Explain your answer.**
(2)

He does not want to be "rich": he says that his father is wealthy from being a banker, "but" his own ambition is to become a lamplighter and "light the lamps" with Leerie.

Some people might be tricked by the fact that the narrator sounds proud of his father's wealth ("as rich as he can be"): they might assume that he wants to be wealthy himself.

The important clue is the word "but". You should say what the narrator wants to do **instead of** becoming rich.

Marking: Needs to say that he does not want to be rich (1 mark) and what he wants to do instead (1 mark).   [2 marks]

---

8.   **(a) List two details from the picture that you do not find in the passage.**   (2)

There are lots of trees.

The lamplighter is hunched over.

Here are some other possibilities:

- Leerie is carrying a stick.
- Leerie wears a hat.
- There are other people in the street.

- The road is paved with large, flat stones.

Any reasonable point is acceptable. This question and the one below are testing your thorough knowledge of the passage (in this case, so that you know what **not** to list), as well as your ability to spot details in the picture.

Marking: 1 mark for each detail.   **[2 marks]**

(b) List two details from the passage that you do not find in the picture.   (2)
The boy is watching from a window.
Maria wants to go to sea.

There are a great many options here.

Just be careful **not to say two very similar things**, which might be counted as the same piece of information – for example, this might only get 1 mark from a harsh marker, because the points relate to the same overall idea:

Tom wants to be a driver.
Maria wants to go to sea.

Marking: 1 mark for each detail.   **[2 marks]**

---

9.   **Would you have liked to be a lamplighter? Using details from the passage or the picture (or both), explain your answer.   (4)**

You could say that you **would not** have wanted to be a lamplighter …

I would not have wanted to be a lamplighter, because I would have had to work "at night", which would have made me tired. Also, I would have had to carry a "ladder" and this would have been difficult: in the picture, the lamplighter is stooped over as he walks.

… or that you **would** have liked to:

I would have liked to be a lamplighter, because it is a peaceful job: in the picture, there are only two people in the road apart from Leerie. Also, I would have been able to make friends as I worked. For example, the narrator knows Leerie's name because the lamplighter comes to his house every night.

Before you plan your answer, find all the key parts of the question:

- There is a direct question ("Would you …?"), which needs a **yes/no answer**.

- You need "details" from the passage and/or the picture. Notice the "s" on "details": you need **more than one detail**.

- You must explain **how these details contribute to your yes/no answer**.

One detail, with a yes/no answer might be worth **3 marks** if the answer is well explained.

Two different details made part of the same point, with a yes/no answer, could be worth **4 marks** if the answer is convincing and it is clear how each piece of evidence supports your argument.

Ideally, however, you want to make **two different points, with a piece of evidence and a clear explanation for each one**.

Notice how the first example answer uses short quotations as evidence. This is the simplest and clearest way to support your ideas. Try to make your quotes as short as possible: one to three words is ideal.

Marking: See discussion above.	**[4 marks]**

END

Blank Page

Paper 3: *The Railway Children*

Roberta (Bobbie) is the oldest of three children. Phyllis is the youngest, and Peter is their brother.

It seemed to her that they had been standing there for hours and hours, holding those silly little red flannel flags that no one would ever notice. The train wouldn't care. It would go rushing by them and tear round the corner and go crashing into that awful mound. And everyone would be killed. Her hands grew very cold and trembled so
5   that she could hardly hold the flag. And then came the distant rumble and hum of the metals, and a puff of white steam showed far away along the stretch of line.

"Stand firm," said Peter, "and wave like mad! When it gets to that big furze bush step back, but go on waving! Don't stand ON the line, Bobbie!"

The train came rattling along very, very
10   fast.

"They don't see us! They won't see us! It's all no good!" cried Bobbie.

The two little flags on the line swayed as the nearing train shook and loosened the
15   heaps of loose stones that held them up. One of them slowly leaned over and fell on the line. Bobbie jumped forward and caught it up, and waved it; her hands did not tremble now.

20   It seemed that the train came on as fast as ever. It was very near now.

"Keep off the line, you silly cuckoo!" said Peter, fiercely.

"It's no good," Bobbie said again.

25   "Stand back!" cried Peter, suddenly, and he dragged Phyllis back by the arm.

Bobbie still waved the flags.

But Bobbie cried, "Not yet, not yet!" and waved her two flags right over the line. The front of the engine looked black and enormous. Its voice was loud and harsh.

"Oh, stop, stop, stop!" cried Bobbie. No one heard her. At least Peter and Phyllis
30   didn't, for the oncoming rush of the train covered the sound of her voice with a mountain of sound. But afterwards she used to wonder whether the engine itself had

not heard her. It seemed almost as though it had – for it slackened swiftly, slackened and stopped, not twenty yards from the place where Bobbie's two flags waved over the line. She saw the great black engine stop dead, but somehow she could not stop

35   waving the flags. And when the driver and the fireman had got off the engine and Peter and Phyllis had gone to meet them and pour out their excited tale of the awful mound just round the corner, Bobbie still waved the flags but more and more feebly and jerkily.

When the others turned towards her she was lying across the line with her hands flung

40   forward and still gripping the sticks of the little red flannel flags.

From *The Railway Children* by E. Nesbit

1. Why does Bobbie think that nobody will "ever notice" their flags (line 2)?

    (1)

....

....

2. **(a)** Write down the sentence from paragraph one that makes the train seem like a person (this is called **personification**). **(1)**

....

    (b) Why do you think the writer talks about the train in this way? **(2)**

....

....

....

....

    (c) There is another short sentence, later in the passage, which also describes the train like a human. Write it down. **(1)**

....

3. Giving evidence from paragraph 1 to back up your points, explain fully why the children are trying to stop the train. **(4)**

....

....

....

....

....

4.   Why will the children have to "step back" (lines 7-8)?   **(2)**

....

....

5.   Why does the writer use the phrase "a mountain of sound" (lines 30-31)?   **(2)**

....

....

....

....

6.   Why do you think Bobbie keeps on waving the flags after the train has stopped (lines 34-38)?   **(2)**

....

....

....

7.   Bobbie is not hit by the train, yet she ends up lying on the tracks. Why do you think this happens?   **(2)**

....

....

....

8.   **(a)** What do you notice about the phrase "slackened swiftly, slackened and stopped" (lines 32-33)?   **(1)**

....

....

(b) Why do you think the writer has written it in this way? **(2)**

....

....

....

9.   Imagine that you are Phyllis, the youngest of the children. Later the same day, you write a letter to a friend in which you talk about what has happened.

What do you think of your sister and brother? Are you proud of yourself?

Use some ideas from the passage in your writing, but be creative as well.   **(5)**

....

....

....

....

....

....

....

....

....

....

....

....

....

....

TOTAL 25

The Railway Children – *Solutions*

Students who struggle with this paper usually do so because they have not spent enough time thinking about the passage. If you do not have a clear understanding of what the three children are trying to do and why, the entire exercise will be confusing.

> **1.   Why does Bobbie think that nobody will "ever notice" their flags (line 2)?**
> **(1)**
>
> She thinks this because they are just "silly little" pieces of cloth.

The answer is easy to write, but there are a few distracting details in the sentence, such as that the flags are "red" and that the children seem to have been there for "hours and hours" – neither of which explains **why the flags might not be noticed**.

Either "silly" or "little" should get the mark. Even if you don't know that "flannel" is a kind of cloth, you can still say that the flags are too small.

- **You don't need to repeat the question**: it would take up most of your answer space! Just be careful to **write a complete sentence**.

> **Marking:** 1 mark for an answer that quotes or explains "silly" or "little".   **[1 mark]**

> **2.   (a) Write down the sentence from paragraph one that makes the train seem like a person (this is called *personification*).** **(1)**
>
> "The train wouldn't care."

Trains can't "care" about things, so this sentence treats the train as though it is actually a person.

You need to read the whole paragraph carefully and not pick a sentence at random! "It would go rushing by them" does not clearly make the train seem like a person, for example.

Be careful to **copy the sentence accurately**.

> **Marking:** Correct answer only.   **[1 mark]**

> **(b) Why do you think the writer talks about the train in this way?** (2)
>
> She is showing us Bobbie's fear, that the train will push past them, like a rude person who ignores people and does not "care" about them.

The important thing is to talk about the **effect** the sentence has – **what it makes the reader** *imagine*.

You have to **talk about the idea of the train being like a person** to get both marks.

- With a question of this sort, which follows on from a previous answer, you can expect to get "follow through" marks. In other words, if you chose the wrong sentence for **(a)**, you can still get the marks for **(b)** if you write intelligently about that incorrect answer.

> **Marking:** Any clear answer that explains why the train might be like a person.
>
> **[2 marks]**

> **(c) There is another short sentence, later in the passage, which also describes the train like a human. Write it down.** (1)
>
> "Its voice was loud and harsh."

You might also get the mark for:

> "But afterwards she used to wonder whether the engine itself had not heard her."

However, this second example is about Bobbie's thoughts – it does not directly describe the train – so the first answer is better.

When you answer a question like this one, you will need to re-read the text (even if you do it quickly). Otherwise you might miss the answer as your eyes scan the page. As you read, make sure that you **underline any possibilities**: it is easy to find something, then lose it again.

> **Marking:** Either of the answers given above. **[1 mark]**

> **3. Giving evidence from paragraph 1 to back up your points, explain fully why the children are trying to stop the train.** (4)
>
> They want to stop it "crashing" into a pile ("mound") on the track, hidden "round the corner". If it crashes, people will be "killed".

Even though there are 4 marks for this question, your answer does not need to be long. You need to explain **what might happen** (the train might crash into an obstacle), and

why this would be a problem (this would cause deaths). You need **evidence** for both points.

Your evidence **does not** need to be given in separate sentences (*point sentence – evidence sentence – point sentence – evidence sentence*). Look at the example to see how **you can put short quotations inside your explanations**, doing two jobs at once.

> **Marking:** 1 mark the fact that the train might crash; 1 mark for the risk of deaths. 1 mark for a piece of evidence to support each point.   **[4 marks]**

> **4.**   **Why will the children have to "step back" (lines 7-8)?**   (2)
>
> This is to stop the train hitting them.

This is worth 2 marks, because there is lots of confusing information in the sentence. Stepping back would not stop the train moving; and it is nothing to do with the "furze" (gorse).

> **Marking:** See example answer (any equivalent point is acceptable). A partly correct answer is worth 1.   **[2 marks]**

> **5.**   **Why does the writer use the phrase "a mountain of sound" (lines 30-31)?**
>   (2)
>
> The train is so loud that you can't hear anything else, like a mountain that is so big you cannot see past it.

You need to say that the sound is loud, and explain a way in which this might relate to the idea of a "mountain". Any sensible way of linking the ideas is fine.

> **Marking:** Up to 2 marks for any sensible answer, clearly explained.   **[2 marks]**

> **6.**   **Why do you think Bobbie keeps on waving the flags after the train has stopped (lines 34-38)?**   (2)
>
> She is so frightened that she cannot think: she just keeps on doing the same thing.

You need to give a reason why she might keep waving (in the example, "she cannot think"), and make clear how it relates to what is happening (for example, because she is "frightened").

> **Marking:** See above. Answers need to be reasonable based on what we know about the situation and Bobbie's character. Far-fetched (but not completely absurd) ideas might be worth 1.   **[2 marks]**

7. **Bobbie is not hit by the train, yet she ends up lying on the tracks. Why do you think this happens?** **(2)**

Because she is exhausted (but also relieved), she faints and falls over.

This just needs a short, sensible explanation, including the idea that Bobbie faints (or collapses from exhaustion) and a reason why. Like in **Question 6**, the wording includes "Why do you think?" which tells you to make up a reasonable answer – even if there isn't enough evidence in the passage to say for sure whether you are right.

Marking: 1 mark for fainting/collapsing; 1 mark for a reasonable explanation of why.
[2 marks]

8. **(a) What do you notice about the phrase "slackened swiftly, slackened and stopped" (lines 32-33)?** **(1)**

It has lots of "s" sounds.

You could also write:

It repeats the word "slackened".

Strictly speaking, you might "notice" that "the phrase is written in English", or that "it contains five words"! However, these answers would not get the mark, because the question is testing your ability to spot **what is interesting or unusual** about the phrase.

An answer relating to rhythm (see **(b)**) would also be acceptable here.

Marking: Any correct answer that relates to an interesting or unusual characteristic. The two examples above are most likely. **[1 mark]**

(b) Why do you think the writer has written it in this way? **(2)**

The following answer focuses on the "s" sounds:

It sounds like the hissing of a steam train coming to a halt.

This focuses on the repetition in the phrase:

The repetition sounds like the rhythm of a train on rails.

A correct answer will almost certainly spot that the sentence sounds like a train. However, there are other possibilities: for example, that it sounds calm, because the danger is over.

Marking: Any sensible, clear explanation such as those above for 2 marks. 1 mark if vaguely reasonable but problematic.   **[2 marks]**

> 9.   **Imagine that you are Phyllis, the youngest of the children. Later the same day, you write a letter to a friend in which you talk about what has happened.**
>
> **What do you think of your sister and brother? Are you proud of yourself?**
>
> **Use some ideas from the passage in your writing, but be creative as well.**
>
> **(5)**
>
> Dear Emma,
>
> I want you to know before you read any more that I would have been a hero too, if it hadn't been for Peter being so bossy and such a coward that he ran away and pulled me with him.
>
> But I haven't told you what happened! We were playing near the railway when I saw a pile of wet stones glistening on the line – they must have rolled down the bank in the rain. Just then, we saw steam tumbling upwards in the distance. We made some flags by ripping up our clothes, and we stood by the track and waved frantically. The train stopped right in front of Bobbie, but she had fallen over so she didn't know.
>
> Now they say we're heroes, which is true (except for that idiot Peter), but especially Bobbie. I'm not very happy about the last bit. It isn't my fault that Peter's bigger than I am.
>
> Love,
>
> Phyllis

The answer space is large so that you can set out your writing in the form of a letter, without running out of room. There is no need to use up all the lines: you don't have to write quite as much as in the example.

Firstly, you need to **do everything the question asks** (this is why you should underline the key words in a question before answering it):

- ✓ It should be a letter of some sort.
- ✓ You should mention your feelings about Bobbie and Peter.
- ✓ You should give your view of yourself.
- ✓ You should include ideas from the passage.

✓ You should use some creative language.

If you miss any of these things out, you might still get the marks – but it is better not to take the risk.

The easiest way to show your creativity with language is to describe some details closely (in the example, "wet stones glistening on the line" and "we saw steam tumbling upwards"). You should aim to give a strong sense of Phyllis's personality.

To make a passage-based piece (such as this letter) seem personal, giving you a chance to draw out the character's feelings, it is a good idea to **identify the moment in the text that is likely to have been most emotional for the character**. You can focus your writing on this. Here, I chose to focus the letter on lines 25-26:

"Stand back!" cried Peter, suddenly, and he dragged Phyllis back by the arm.

Both the first and last paragraphs of the example mention this incident.

You will lose marks in creative writing questions if you make too many mistakes with your English, so always check your answer carefully. In particular, make sure that you have used full stops, capital letters, commas and speech marks in the right places.

> **Marking:** A 5-mark answer will be closely based on the characters and events in the story, giving an imaginative but believable idea of how Phyllis might react to them. It will use a good proportion of the answer space, and will include a wide variety of interesting language. It will have very few English errors: if there are any, they will be minor. Use your judgement to subtract marks if elements of the above are missing. Marks below 3 should only be awarded if an answer is very weak. **[5 marks]**

END

Blank Page

Paper 4: *The Pobble Who Has No Toes*

Edward Lear was an extraordinarily talented man – a magnificent painter, alongside his work as a poet and author and in other fields. His 'nonsense poems' often conceal serious ideas and deep emotions.

The Pobble who has no toes
Had once as many as we;
When they said "Some day you may lose them all";
He replied "Fish, fiddle-de-dee!"
5 And his Aunt Jobiska made him drink
Lavender water tinged with pink,
For she said "The World in general knows
There's nothing so good for a Pobble's toes!"

The Pobble who has no toes
10 Swam across the Bristol Channel;
But before he set out he wrapped his nose
In a piece of scarlet flannel.
For his Aunt Jobiska said "No harm
Can come to his toes if his nose is warm;
15 And it's perfectly known that a Pobble's toes
Are safe, – provided he minds his nose!"

The Pobble swam fast and well,
And when boats or ships came near him,
He tinkledy-blinkledy-winkled a bell,
20 So that all the world could hear him.
And all the Sailors and Admirals cried,
When they saw him nearing the further side –
"He has gone to fish for his Aunt Jobiska's
Runcible Cat with crimson whiskers!"

But before he touched the shore,
The shore of the Bristol Channel,
A sea-green porpoise carried away
His wrapper of scarlet flannel.
And when he came to observe his feet,
Formerly garnished with toes so neat,
His face at once became forlorn,
On perceiving that all his toes were gone!

And nobody ever knew,
From that dark day to the present,
35   Whoso had taken the Pobble's toes,
In a manner so far from pleasant.
Whether the shrimps, or crawfish grey,
Or crafty Mermaids stole them away –
Nobody knew: and nobody knows
40   How the Pobble was robbed of his twice five toes!

The Pobble who has no toes
Was placed in a friendly Bark,
And they rowed him back, and carried him up
To his Aunt Jobiska's Park.
45   And she made him a feast at his earnest wish
Of eggs and buttercups fried with fish, -
And she said "It's a fact the whole world knows,
That Pobbles are happier without their toes!"

By Edward Lear

1. Write down the meanings of the following words, as they are used in the text:

    (a) tinged (line 6)   ……………………………………

    (b) forlorn (line 31)   ……………………………………

    (c) crafty (line 38)   ……………………………………

    (d) bark (line 42)   ……………………………………   **(4)**

2. **(a)** Why does the Pobble say "Fish, fiddle-de-dee!" (line 4)?

    A   He thinks it is time to go fishing.
    B   He doesn't believe what Aunt Jobiska has told him.
    C   He doesn't much care about his toes.
    D   He has misheard what Aunt Jobiska said.
    E   He is thinking of playing his fiddle (violin).

                                    Answer: …………… **(1)**

    (b) What does this suggest about his personality?   **(2)**

    ………………………………………………………………………………………………

    ………………………………………………………………………………………………

    ………………………………………………………………………………………………

3. What is meant by "the World in general" (line 7)?

    A   Some people
    B   People in the army
    C   The planet earth
    D   Well-informed people
    E   Most people

                                    Answer: …………… **(1)**

4.   Why does the Pobble wrap "his nose / In a piece of scarlet flannel" (lines 11-
12)? Use your own words as far as you can.   **(2)**

....

....

....

5.   Write down three different colours named in the passage.   **(3)**

        (i)   ....

        (ii)   ....

        (iii)   ....

6.   Explain the phrase "dark day" (line 34).   **(1)**

....

....

7.   What sort of a person is Aunt Jobiska? Make at least two points about her
personality, explaining why you believe each thing.   **(4)**

....

....

....

....

....

....

8.   **(a)** How many toes did the Pobble have before his accident?

    A   10
    B   0
    C   5
    D   9
    E   20

Answer: .... **(1)**

    (b) Write down the numbers of two lines that suggest this to you.   **(2)**

    (i)   ....

    (ii)   ....

9.   Try to imagine what a "Runcible Cat" (line 24) might be. Describe it as fully as you can.

    You do not need to base your answer on evidence from the passage.   **(4)**

....

....

....

....

....

....

....

....

TOTAL 25

The Pobble Who Has No Toes – *Solutions*

The questions in this paper are not too difficult, but the passage offers some challenges.

For one thing, it is fairly long, meaning that important details can be tricky to find.

What's more, the ideas and the language are not always easy. Some people engage instinctively with nonsense, and like the imaginative freedom that it allows; others find the weird words and ridiculous situations off-putting, because they make it difficult to be sure what is correct and what is not.

<table>
<tr><td>1.</td><td colspan="2">Write down the meanings of the following words, as they are used in the text.
(4)</td></tr>
<tr><td></td><td>(a) tinged (line 6)</td><td>coloured / tinted</td></tr>
<tr><td></td><td>(b) forlorn (line 31)</td><td>sad</td></tr>
<tr><td></td><td>(c) crafty (line 38)</td><td>cunning</td></tr>
<tr><td></td><td>(d) bark (line 42)</td><td>boat</td></tr>
</table>

All of these look like difficult words, but in fact it is possible to **work each one out from its context** (the ideas around it).

For example, the word "bark" might trick you because it sounds like the outside of a tree; but if you see that the Pobble is "placed" in it, then "rowed" back, it becomes obvious that this must be some kind of **boat**.

Sometimes it is helpful to **find the word in the passage and cover it with your thumb**, so that you aren't misled by its sound or appearance: ask yourself what word might go best in the concealed place. Then look at the word again, and decide whether you are happy with your idea.

A sensible (but wrong) answer might still get half a mark.

Marking: 1 mark for each correct answer. Accept near equivalents. A wrong guess that nevertheless makes sense in the poem is worth 0.5 marks.   **[4 marks]**

> **2.** **(a) Why does the Pobble say "Fish, fiddle-de-dee!" (line 4)?** (1)
>
> ~~A   He thinks it is time to go fishing.~~
> **B**   He doesn't believe what Aunt Jobiska has told him.
> **C**   He doesn't care about his toes.
> **D**   He has misheard what Aunt Jobiska said.
> ~~E   He is thinking of playing his fiddle (violin).~~
>
> **Answer: B**

Don't be tricked by the word "fish" into thinking that fish should be somewhere in your answer (**A**)!

E is also not likely.

   ✓ Notice that I cross out **A** and **E**, enabling me to concentrate on the more realistic options.

Because this question asks "why" the Pobble says something, but the passage doesn't give the answer, you need to **imagine yourself in his position**:

> *What would it mean if an adult gave you a warning, and you just said "Fish fiddle-de-dee"?*

Of course, it would sound rude. So **why** is he being rude?

   ✓ When you must imagine yourself saying or doing what a character does, so that you can picture their feelings, comprehension is quite like acting!

B, **C** and **D** are all *possible*, but you have to choose the *best*/most likely answer.

C is less likely than **B**: it is usual for a person to care about having their toes (or other body parts) removed, even though we can't completely rule **C** out.

D *could* be true, but there is no evidence that he has misheard Aunt Jobiska.

B, however, makes perfect sense. The Pobble's reaction is typical of a person who has been given a warning that they simply don't take seriously.

> *Imagine your likely response if somebody says "Remember to take your umbrella!" as you leave the house on a cloudless, sunny day.*

Marking: B   [1 mark]

> **(b) What does this suggest about his personality?**   **(2)**
>
> The Pobble doesn't like to think about the future. Also, he is somebody who can be rude to others: he is inconsiderate.

This comes from imagining that you are the Pobble. **What sort of person would you have to be**, to say this to your aunt?

It is important to **notice the number of marks**. If you make two short points, this is the safest way to get both marks; another option is to make a single point, but explain it thoroughly.

Any sensible ideas will be marked as correct.

> **Marking:** See discussion. Ideas must be relevant to the quote from **(a)**.   **[2 marks]**

> 3.   **What is meant by "the World in general" (line 7)?**   **(1)**
>
>   A   ~~Some people~~
>   B   ~~People in the army~~
>   C   The planet earth
>   D   ~~Well-informed people~~
>   E   Most people
>
>   **Answer: E**

B depends on a big misunderstanding of the word "general", and can be crossed out first.

Meanwhile, **A** and **D** ignore the clear meaning of "in general", which is similar to "most" or even "all".

Because Jobiska refers to what "the World ... **knows**", this must be a reference to **people** rather than the planet on which they stand – meaning that **E** is the right answer.

> **Marking: E**   **[1 mark]**

---

4. **Why does the Pobble wrap "his nose / In a piece of scarlet flannel" (lines 11-12)? Use your own words as far as you can.** **(2)**

He does this because his aunt says that his toes will be protected as long as his nose stays cosy.

If you have read the passage carefully, you will realise that the answer to this question can be found in lines 13-16.

This question asks you to **use your own words**, in order to test that you understand what is going on in the text. If you use a few of the words from the passage, this is not a disaster – **so long as they do not represent the most important ideas**.

However, an answer that repeats, for example, "No harm can come to his toes if his toes are warm", can only get 1 mark: this is the right information, but because you have not put it in your own words, it is possible that you do not fully understand what it means.

Marking: 1 mark for correct answer. 2 marks if also written well, using own words.
[2 marks]

---

5. **Write down three different colours named in the passage.** **(3)**

(i) pink

(ii) scarlet

(iii) crimson

"Sea-green", "green" and "grey" are also options.

However, "dark" is not a colour.

Marking: 1 mark for each correct colour (from the six options listed above). **[3 marks]**

---

6. **Explain the phrase "dark day" (line 34).** **(1)**

It is a sad day, because the Pobble has lost his toes.

It is important to understand that the day <u>might not actually be dark</u>. The phrase is saying that this is **a bad day for the Pobble**: it is a **metaphor** (a way of writing one thing, while meaning something else).

Marking: Needs to say that it is a sad/terrible (or similar) day. Doesn't need to say why.
[1 mark]

---

7.   What sort of a person is Aunt Jobiska? Make at least two points about her personality, explaining why you believe each thing.   (4)

She is wise, because she knows that the Pobble's toes might be at risk if he removes his flannel. This is proved right by events. She is also very positive-minded: after the Pobble has lost his toes, she says that he will be "happier".

It is essential to talk about Jobiska's **personality**: what "sort of a person" she is. The danger is that you will say that she is a woman, or that she is the Pobble's aunt: neither of these would count!

The question tells you to "make at least two points". There are 4 marks available, which means that two points (with you explaining why you believe each thing, based on the poem) will be enough.

✓ If you are able to make another point, your answer will be even safer.

The process for answering this sort of question is as follows:

1.   Find **three or four things that Aunt Jobiska says or does**. <u>Underline</u> each one (e.g. "Pobbles are happier without their toes").

2.   **Work out what each one suggests about her personality/character**. Note your ideas down alongside the text (e.g. "very positive").

3.   From your ideas, **choose two or three that are very different from each other** (so you don't accidentally make the same point twice). The example uses two.

4.   **Write** your answer, **explaining** how each piece of evidence supports each point.

The following answer **would not get full marks**:

Aunt Jobiska is kind, because she wants the Pobble to keep his toes safe. She is also caring, because she wants him to be "happier".

Do you see the problem?

This answer seems to be making two different points, but in fact (by saying that Jobiska is "kind" and "caring") it is essentially making the same point twice. It would get 2 or 3 marks out of 4.

Marking: See discussion.   **[4 marks]**

---

8.   **(a) How many toes did the Pobble have before his accident?**   **(1)**

        A   10

        B   0

        C   5

        D   9

        E   20

                                                          Answer: **A**

    (b) Write down the numbers of two lines that suggest this to you.   **(2)**

    (i)   2

    (ii)   40

Line 2 might be confusing (*Is it talking about five toes or ten? What if for any reason you do not have ten toes yourself?*), but line 40 says "twice five", which should make things clear.

The main cause of confusion here is likely to be the title. Although he has "no toes" *now*, this does not tell you how many toes the Pobble had *before* his accident.

Marking: Correct answers only.   **[1 mark for (a), 2 marks for (b)]**

9.   **Try to imagine what a "Runcible Cat" (line 24) might be. Describe it as fully as you can.**

You do not need to base your answer on evidence from the passage.   **(4)**

Its face is round, as large as a frying pan, and dips in the middle around its nose and below its third eye, which sits in the middle of its forehead. Its fur is thick as moss and nearly as soggy (because it licks itself a lot), and grey, almost blue – except for its crimson whiskers, which glow slightly in the dark. It likes to stay very still on top of Aunt Jobiska's wardrobe, but its eyes follow you. It is rather fat, and its purr makes the furniture vibrate.

Try to give the marker **at least four things** to tick.

Because this is a very unusual cat (with a strange name and odd-coloured whiskers), the best answers will probably think about the ways in which it is **strange** (its "third eye", in the example), but also the ways in which – being a cat – it is **familiar** (it purrs loudly "on top of Aunt Jobiska's wardrobe"). Aim to write descriptively, perhaps by using adjectives ("soggy") and a variety of verbs.

This is a creative writing question, so you might lose a mark if you make too many English mistakes: always re-read your work carefully, out loud if you can.

Marking: 1 mark per good idea – or 2 marks, if an idea is very well developed. However, only award 4 marks if the answer is creative: well written, with some interesting descriptive language. Deduct marks for significant (or multiple) English errors.   **[4 marks]**

END

Paper 5: *The War of the Worlds*

A large object ("the cylinder") has fallen from space and crashed into the ground near London. As a crowd gathers, something inside the cylinder begins to move.

When I returned to the common the sun was setting. Scattered groups were hurrying from the direction of Woking, and one or two persons were returning. The crowd about the pit had increased, and stood out black against the lemon yellow of the sky – a couple of hundred people, perhaps. There were raised voices, and some sort of
5   struggle appeared to be going on about the pit. Strange imaginings passed through my mind. As I drew nearer I heard Stent's voice:

"Keep back! Keep back!"

A boy came running towards me.

"It's a-movin'," he said to me as he passed; "a-screwin' and a-screwin' out. I don't like
10   it. I'm a-goin' 'ome, I am."

I went on to the crowd. There were really, I should think, two or three hundred people elbowing and jostling one another, the one or two ladies there being by no means the least active.

"He's fallen in the pit!" cried someone.

15   "Keep back!" said several.

The crowd swayed a little, and I elbowed my way through. Everyone seemed greatly excited. I heard a peculiar humming sound from the pit.

"I say!" said Ogilvy; "help keep these idiots back. We don't know what's in the confounded thing, you know!"

20   I saw a young man, a shop assistant in Woking I believe he was, standing on the cylinder and trying to scramble out of the hole again. The crowd had pushed him in.

The end of the cylinder was being screwed out from within. Nearly two feet of shining screw projected. Somebody blundered against me, and I narrowly missed being pitched onto the top of the screw. I turned, and as I did so the screw must have come
25   out, for the lid of the cylinder fell upon the gravel with a ringing concussion. I stuck my elbow into the person behind me, and turned my head towards the Thing again. For a moment that circular cavity seemed perfectly black. I had the sunset in my eyes.

I think everyone expected to see a man emerge – possibly something a little unlike us terrestrial men, but in all essentials a man. I know I did. But, looking, I presently saw
30   something stirring within the shadow: greyish billowy movements, one above

another, and then two luminous disks – like eyes. Then something resembling a little grey snake, about the thickness of a walking stick, coiled up out of the writhing middle, and wriggled in the air towards me – and then another.

35 A sudden chill came over me. There was a loud shriek from a woman behind. I half turned, keeping my eyes fixed upon the cylinder still, from which other tentacles were now projecting, and began pushing my way back from the edge of the pit. I saw astonishment giving place to horror on the faces of the people about me. I heard inarticulate exclamations on all sides. There was a general movement backwards. I saw the shopman struggling still on the edge of the pit. I found myself alone, and saw

40 the people on the other side of the pit running off, Stent among them. I looked again at the cylinder, and ungovernable terror gripped me. I stood petrified and staring.

A big greyish rounded bulk, the size, perhaps, of a bear, was rising slowly and painfully out of the cylinder. As it bulged up and caught the light, it glistened like wet leather.

45 Two large dark-coloured eyes were regarding me steadfastly. The mass that framed them, the head of the thing, was rounded, and had, one might say, a face. There was a mouth under the eyes, the lipless brim of which quivered and panted, and dropped saliva.

From *The War of the Worlds* by H.G. Wells

1.   At what time of day is the story set?   **(1)**

……………………………………………………………………………………………

2.   Write down two words that describe the way the crowd moves, from lines 11-
      16. What does each of these words suggest about the crowd?   **(4)**

Word 1:   …………………………..

Explanation: …………………..………………………………………………………

Word 2:   …………………………..

Explanation: …………………………………………………………………………..

3.   Why does Ogilvy want to "keep these idiots back" (line 18)?   **(2)**

……………………………………………………………………………………………

……………………………………………………………………………………………

……………………………………………………………………………………………

4.   Why do you think the crowd has "pushed" the young shop assistant into the
      hole (line 21)?   **(2)**

……………………………………………………………………………………………

……………………………………………………………………………………………

……………………………………………………………………………………………

5.   Explain in your own words why the hole seems "perfectly black" to the
      narrator (the main character) in line 27.   **(2)**

……………………………………………………………………………………………

……………………………………………………………………………………………

……………………………………………………………………………………………

6.   What did people expect to see emerge from the cylinder?   **(1)**

....

....

7.   Write down the meanings of the following words, as they are used in the passage: **(4)**

(a) luminous (line 31)   ....

(b) tentacles (line 35)   ....

(c) ungovernable (line 41)   ....

(d) petrified (line 41)   ....

8.   How does the writer make the text scary, up to line 27? Make at least two points, and explain your ideas by giving information from the passage.   **(4)**

....

....

....

....

....

....

9.   How large is the alien?   **(1)**

....

10. Using your own words as far as possible, describe the alien's appearance (how it looks). **(4)**

....

....

....

....

....

....

TOTAL 25

The War of the Worlds – *Solutions*

These questions do not present any unusual challenges, but the passage is long and the situation is bewildering: it is told from the point of view of a narrator who is very confused, and it describes the behaviour of excited, scared people whose actions are difficult to explain. Questions 8 and 10 need developed answers and will require a bit of extra thought.

---

1. At what time of day is the story set?	**(1)**
It is the evening, at sunset.	

Either part of the example – "the evening" or "sunset" – is fine.

It would not be correct to say that the story is set at night or in the afternoon (although "late afternoon" would probably be acceptable).

Marking: Any answer that refers to the evening or sunset.   **[1 mark]**

---

2. Write down two words that describe the way the crowd moves, from lines 11-16. What does each of these words suggest about the crowd?	**(4)**
Word 1: elbowing	
Explanation: People are excited, pushing each other.	
Word 2: swayed	
Explanation: The whole crowd shifts together, from side to side.	

You could also use "jostling".

Any sensible explanation is fine, so long as it talks about **the crowd**, rather than an individual person.

When explaining a quotation, **don't just repeat the main idea in a slightly different way**. You have to find a new way to make it clear.

- For example, if you wrote that "swayed" shows how "the crowd swayed from side to side", you wouldn't make things any clearer!

Marking: 1 mark each for two of "elbowing", "swayed" and "jostling". 1 mark for each sensible explanation that focuses on the crowd as a whole.   **[4 marks]**

---

3.   Why does Ogilvy want to "keep these idiots back" (line 18)?   (2)

This is because they "don't know" what is in the cylinder and it might be dangerous.

The main point is that they don't know what is inside. To get 2 marks, you need to **add some extra explanation**: *why* does not knowing what is in the cylinder mean that the people have to stay back?

Alternatively, you could explain why Ogilvy calls the people 'idiots':

They "don't know" what is in the cylinder, but the "idiots" are pushing each other towards to it.

Any clear and sensible explanation should be fine here.

Marking: 1 mark for explaining that they don't know what's there. 1 mark for an extra point or a development of the idea.   **[2 marks]**

- -

---

4.   Why do you think the crowd has "pushed" the young shop assistant into the hole (line 21)?   (2)

I imagine they have knocked him in by accident, because everybody is so desperate to get close and see.

Your answer needs to be **a reasonable response to ideas in the text**: the example answer is based on the fact that the crowd is "excited" and "jostling". The following answer would <u>not</u> be good, because there is no evidence in the text to support it:

I expect he was pushed in by bullies, perhaps because he was annoying them.

When you see wording like "Why do you think … ?" you need to be prepared to use your imagination – but also keep a close eye on the information in the passage.

Marking: A reasonable and clearly explained response. An answer that isn't clearly explained, or is unlikely, might be worth 1 mark.   **[2 marks]**

- -

---

5.   Explain in your own words why the hole seems "perfectly black" to the narrator (the main character) in line 27.   (2)

The sun is dazzling him (it is low in the sky), so everything else seems dark by comparison.

There is 1 mark for recognizing that it is to do with the sunset, or at least the sun, and another for explaining: either that **it is dazzling him**, or that **it creates a contrast**. The example includes both options.

Marking: See above.   **[2 marks]**

6.	What did people expect to see emerge from the cylinder?	(1)
They expected to see "a man", or something very similar.		

'A man' is the important information, and should be enough for the mark. However, the example also touches on the suggestion, in lines 28-29, that this man might not be quite like men from Earth.

Marking: 1 mark for a man/person, or for saying that they expect something like a person. **[1 mark]**

7.	Write down the meanings of the following words, as they are used in the passage:	(4)
(a) **luminous (line 31)** shining		
(b) **tentacles (line 35)** long arms		
(c) **ungovernable (line 41)** uncontrollable		
(d) **petrified (line 41)** frozen / turned to stone		

You have to **read the information <u>around</u> a word** in order to work out its meaning – particularly because you have to identify the meaning "in the passage".

Cover the word, and work out what idea is most likely to belong in the gap: then see whether this makes sense, looking again at the original word to check.

If you put something sensible but wrong, you might still get half a mark.

Marking: 1 mark for each correct answer. 0.5 marks for each partly correct answer.
[4 marks]

> **8.** **How does the writer make the text scary, up to line 27? Make at least two points, and explain your ideas by giving information from the passage.** **(4)**
>
> Firstly, the lid of the cylinder is "screwed out" slowly, for a long time, which builds suspense: like the crowd, we must wait before we discover whether the thing inside is dangerous. Secondly, the man who is "trying to scramble out" seems trapped, and nobody seems to be helping him. We can imagine how scared he must be.

Look through the text for two scary moments. Ideally you should find more, then choose the best and most different two to write about. Then try to work out what is frightening about them. You need to **explain properly how each one is scary**. In the example answer, the words "suspense" and "trapped" help to achieve this.

Make sure that you make **two separate points**, each one with **its own evidence** (probably a quote): don't cut corners.

> **Marking:** 1 mark each for two relevant examples from the passage. 1 mark each for clear and convincing explanations of why the examples are scary. **[4 marks]**

> **9.** **How large is the alien?** **(1)**
>
> It is about the size of "a bear".

So long as your answer shows that the alien is roughly bear-sized (for example, *the alien is about 1.5 metres tall*), it should be marked as correct.

> **Marking:** See above. **[1 mark]**

> **10.** **Using your own words as far as possible, describe the alien's appearance (how it looks).** **(4)**
>
> It is large and baggy, quite like a ball, and about the size of a small car. It is shiny, and it dribbles from its wobbly mouth, which has no lips. Its eyes are dark but they reflect some light. It has many tentacles, each of them a couple of centimetres thick.

You are likely to get 4 marks if you write about **four different features of the alien** and **use you own words** most of the time.

However, you might **not** get extra marks for making several points about **a single part of the creature's appearance**: the example makes three points about the mouth, but it probably wouldn't earn 3 marks for these alone (they might be enough for 2).

- Before answering the question, look at the passage again and **underline important information** about the alien's appearance.

- Once you have done this, work out **how you would explain each idea to somebody sitting opposite you**.

When a question asks for your "own words", be careful not to repeat things from the passage. You need to show a strong grasp of what everything means: if you repeat a word it might be because you don't fully understand it. However, don't worry if you re-use basic words for which there isn't a clear alternative.

The example makes more points than it has to, which is often a sensible thing to do if you have time, to make certain of your marks.

Marking: 1 mark for each of four different features of the alien. Subtract up to 2 marks if use of own words is poor or absent.   **[4 marks]**

END

Paper 6:
Coldtonguecoldhamcoldbeefpickledgherkinssaladfrenchrollscre sssandwichespottedmeatgingerbeerlemonadesodawater

On a beautiful spring day, the Mole leaves his hole and goes for a walk. He bumps into the Water Rat, who invites him to come on a boat trip. The word "scull" means "oar" (noun) or "row" (verb): when somebody "sculls", they are rowing.

"Do you know, I've never been in a boat before in all my life."

"What?" cried the Rat, open-mouthed: "Never been in a—you never—well I—what have you been doing, then?"

"Is it so nice as all that?" asked the Mole shyly, though he was quite prepared to
5 believe it as he leant back in his seat and surveyed the cushions, the oars, the rowlocks, and all the fascinating fittings, and felt the boat sway lightly under him.

"Nice? It's the ONLY thing," said the Water Rat solemnly, as he leant forward for his stroke. "Believe me, my young friend, there is NOTHING—absolutely nothing—half so much worth doing as simply messing about in boats. Simply messing," he went on
10 dreamily: "messing—about—in—boats; messing——"

"Look ahead, Rat!" cried the Mole suddenly.

It was too late. The boat struck the bank full tilt. The dreamer, the joyous oarsman, lay on his back at the bottom of the boat, his heels in the air.

"—about in boats—or WITH boats," the Rat went on composedly, picking himself up
15 with a pleasant laugh. "In or out of 'em, it doesn't matter. Nothing seems really to matter, that's the charm of it. Whether you get away, or whether you don't; whether you arrive at your destination or whether you reach somewhere else, or whether you never get anywhere at all, you're always busy, and you never do anything in particular; and when you've done it there's always something else to do, and you can
20 do it if you like, but you'd much better not. Look here! If you've really nothing else on hand this morning, supposing we drop down the river together, and have a long day of it?"

The Mole waggled his toes from sheer happiness, spread his chest with a sigh of full contentment, and leant back blissfully into the soft cushions. "WHAT a day I'm
25 having!" he said. "Let us start at once!"

"Hold hard a minute, then!" said the Rat. He looped the painter through a ring in his landing-stage, climbed up into his hole above, and after a short interval reappeared staggering under a fat, wicker luncheon-basket.

"Shove that under your feet," he observed to the Mole, as he passed it down into the boat. Then he untied the painter and took the sculls again.

"What's inside it?" asked the Mole, wriggling with curiosity.

"There's   cold   chicken   inside   it,"   replied   the   Rat   briefly; "coldtonguecoldhamcoldbeefpickledgherkinssaladfrenchrollscresssandwichespotted meatgingerbeerlemonadesodawater——"

"O stop, stop," cried the Mole in delight: "This is too much!"

"Do you really think so?" enquired the Rat seriously. "It's only what I always take on these little excursions."

The Mole never heard a word he was saying. He trailed a paw in the water and dreamed long waking dreams. The Water Rat, like the good little fellow he was, sculled steadily on and did not disturb him.

"I like your clothes awfully, old chap," he remarked after some half an hour or so had passed. "I'm going to get a black velvet smoking-suit myself some day, as soon as I can afford it."

"I beg your pardon," said the Mole, pulling himself together with an effort. "You must think me very rude; but all this is so new to me. So—this—is—a—River!"

"THE River," corrected the Rat.

Adapted from *The Wind in the Willows*, by Kenneth Grahame

1. "Never been in a—you never—well I—what have you been doing, then?"

    (a) What is unusual about this sentence? **(1)**

    ....

    ....

    (b) Why do you think it has been written in this way? **(2)**

    ....

    ....

    ....

2. **(a)** Why is the Mole "shy" in line 4? **(2)**

    ....

    ....

    (b) Why is the Mole "prepared to believe" that being in boats might be "so nice"? Give two different reasons, based on the information in lines 5-6. **(2)**

    ....

    ....

    ....

    ....

3.   Why are some of the Rat's words (for example in lines 7-8) written in capital letters?   **(2)**

....

....

....

4.   Give two reasons why lines 33-34 are written as they are. Explain your points.
                                                                                                        (3)

....

....

....

....

....

5.   Basing your answer on lines 15-20, why does Rat like "messing about in boats"?
                                                                                                        (2)

....

....

....

....

6.   What does the word "excursions" mean in line 37?   **(1)**

....

7.   "He trailed a paw in the water and dreamed long waking dreams." Re-write this sentence (from lines 38-39) in your own words.   **(3)**

....

....

8.   What makes the Mole think that he has been "rude" (line 45)?   **(1)**

....

....

9.   Give a reason why you think the Rat calls this "THE river" in line 46.   **(1)**

....

....

10. Write the first few lines of a later chapter, in which the Rat goes to visit the Mole's tunnel for the first time.

Describe the scene, and imagine how the Rat might react to this new place. **(5)**

....

....

....

....

....

....

....

....

....

....

....

....

....

....

....

TOTAL 25

Blank Page

Coldtonguecoldhamcoldbeefpickledgherkinssaladfrenchrolls cresssandwichespottedmeatgingerbeerlemonadesodawater – *Solutions*

The passage includes a lot of speech, some of it in quite complex sentences, and at times the vocabulary is challenging. The questions often ask you to discuss the ways in which things are written, rather than just requiring you to find and explain information.

---

1. **"Never been in a—you never—well I—what have you been doing, then?"**

(a) What is unusual about this sentence? **(1)**

It keeps stopping and starting again.

You could also write that it repeats "never", or that it is full of dashes.

To get the mark, you need to:

- show an understanding of what might be "unusual";
- write an answer based on the sentence itself, not on other things in the passage.

Marking: See discussion. **[1 mark]**

(b) Why do you think it has been written in this way? **(2)**

The Rat keeps pausing, because he is so amazed that the Mole has never been in a boat.

You need to explain how the Rat is speaking (in the example, "the Rat keeps pausing"), for 1 mark.

As well as this, you can either explain **how your answer to part (a) shows this**, or say **why the Rat is feeling this way** – for the second mark.

Marking: See discussion. **[2 marks]**

2. **(a) Why is the Mole "shy" in line 4?** (2)

He is embarrassed that he seems ignorant, because he has never been in a boat.

Another answer might be:

He is shy about admitting how much he likes being in the boat.

There may be other possibilities!

This is tricky because the answer is not stated in the passage. You have to imagine that you are the character, and (looking for clues in the text) imagine what he is thinking, trying to work out what has made him feel this way.

Some clues might be that the Rat is "open-mouthed" that the Mole has "never been in a boat", or that the Mole asks whether it is really "so nice".

The next step is to write a clear explanation.

Marking: Either 1 mark for the emotional background (not repeating "shy" – e.g. he is embarrassed) and 1 mark for a reason – **or** 2 marks for a clear explanation (e.g. the second example). **[2 marks]**

(b) Why is the Mole "prepared to believe" that being in boats might be "so nice"? Give two different reasons, based on the information in lines 5-6. (2)

The boat is full of "fascinating" things, and it sways "lightly".

"Prepared to believe" might be difficult, but part of the challenge here is to look past the awkward words and find the main information in lines 5-6.

You have to apply a dose of common sense to a question like this, and not just respond robotically. Two different features of the boat (e.g. the "cushions" and the "fittings") would not be worth 2 marks, because **they are part of the same overall reason why the Mole is happy**: the boat contains interesting, beautiful things.

The ideal technique for a question such as this is to **underline several points** in 5-6, then **choose the two most different ones**.

Marking: 1 mark for each reason, so long as they are clearly different. **[2 marks]**

3.   **Why are some of the Rat's words (for example in lines 7-8) written in capital letters?** **(2)**

When he is excited by an idea he becomes quite serious, and says some words more loudly, with extra emphasis.

Any sensible explanation is fine here. However, a simple explanation (for example, that he says these words more loudly) might not be enough for 2 marks unless you explain it well. See how the example fleshes out this idea.

Marking: A well explained idea that makes sense, or two brief ideas.   **[2 marks]**

4.   **Give two reasons why lines 33-34 are written as they are. Explain your points.** **(3)**

Firstly, the Rat is talking quickly because he is excited, so the words run together. Secondly, the list shows how many things there are in the basket: the words are crammed together like the food, without space in between.

Some **likely mistakes** here include:

- saying **how** the lines are written, but not **why**;
- making two points that are **versions of the same idea**.

Before answering, you need to **imagine the Rat saying these words**, and consider **how he must be feeling**.

Marking: 1 mark for each reason. An extra mark for some extra explanation of one reason, if clear. **[3 marks]**

5.   **Basing your answer on lines 15-20, why does Rat like "messing about in boats"?** **(2)**

Even if you don't get far, there is lots to do in the boat – but none of it is very important, so there is nothing to worry about.

Just saying that nothing matters, or that you never do anything in particular, might not be enough: to be safe, you need to explain (at least partly) **why** these are good things – **why Rat likes them**.

- This is because having nothing to do could easily also be a bad thing.

When a question asks you to base your answer on a lengthy section (here, six lines), it is very important to **find the main ideas**. If you simply copy out lengthy quotes, you won't get a good number of marks, because this way you won't show that you understand the key points.

Marking: 1 mark for "lots to do" or similar, 1 mark for "no worries"/"nothing is important" etc. (if clear).   **[2 marks]**

---

6.   What does the word "excursions" mean in line 37?   **(1)**

It means "journeys" or "trips".

You may not know the word already, but the question is testing your ability to **think logically** about language.

✓ The best approach is to cover the word, and work out what could go in the space instead:

"It's only what I always take on these little _____."

Marking: See example – or an equivalent answer.   **[1 mark]**

---

7.   "He trailed a paw in the water and dreamed long waking dreams." Re-write this sentence (from lines 38-39) in your own words.   **(3)**

The Mole dragged his hand over the edge of the boat and daydreamed for some time.

"Trailed a paw" and "dreamed long waking dreams" are the key things – any sensible re-working of these is likely to get 3 marks.

When a question asks you to re-write something in your own words, you need to **underline** each idea, **think about how you might say each one** to show that you understand it, then **put your ideas together** in a good order.

Here is the thought process that produced the example answer:

He trailed a paw in the water and dreamed long waking dreams.

He trailed a paw in the water and dreamed long waking dreams.

he – the Mole

trailed – dragged

a paw – his hand

in the water – over the edge of the boat

dreamed long waking dreams – daydreamed for some time

This gives:

> The Mole <u>dragged</u> <u>his hand</u> <u>over the edge of the boat</u> and <u>daydreamed for some</u> <u>time</u>.

Marking: 3 marks for an answer with the main ideas ("trailed a paw", and "dreamed long waking dreams"), convincingly in own words. Subtract marks for missing elements or excessive use of words from the text.   **[3 marks]**

---

8.   What makes the Mole think that he has been "rude" (line 45)?   **(1)**

He has been daydreaming for half an hour and ignoring the Rat.

This might be confusing, because the answer is to be found **a few lines before line 45**.

✓ This is a good reason for **reading the passage thoroughly** before starting work (perhaps more than once), so that you have a sense of what information is where.

Either part of the example answer would probably be enough by itself.

Marking: Either of the two ideas in the example.   **[1 mark]**

---

9.   Give a reason why you think the Rat calls this "THE river" in line 46.   **(1)**

For him, it is the most important river in the world.

Any sensible answer that gives a reason why he says this **with emphasis** will do. You need to notice that this is **not just any old river**.

However, **<u>the following answers would not be correct</u>**, because they don't deal with why he "**calls**" it this: like **Question 3**, they deal with why capitals are used.

It is because he is talking loudly.

But why does he say **this particular word** loudly?

He talks like this because he thinks this is an important thing to say.

But **why** does he think it is important?

Marking: See discussion.	[1 mark]

10.	Write the first few lines of a later chapter, in which the Rat goes to visit the Mole's tunnel for the first time.

10. Write the first few lines of a later chapter, in which the Rat goes to visit the Mole's tunnel for the first time.

Describe the scene, and imagine how the Rat might react to this new place.

(5)

"Well I say!" exclaimed the Rat. "This is quite the most CHARMING ... Ow!"

"Are you alright back there, old thing?" called the Mole over his shoulder.

"And how do you keep your fur clean, down here?" inquired the Rat, undaunted – "With all this soil? And no river?"

But Mole was not listening. He was lost in the joy of home. He pulled open a cupboard and admired the ranks of polished brasses that winked back at him in the candlelight, just where he had left them.

From somewhere along the hall, Mole heard a sharp "thump". He sighed and turned. "Your flooring is SENSATIONAL," declared the Rat. "You've rolled it so firm – it's like the hull of a boat."

Your answer must be interesting, and it must show Rat's reaction to this strange place. It is best to write in the third person ("he"/ "the Rat"), because this is what the passage does.

These things would also help:

✓ A strong sense of **the characters** and **how they tend to behave**.

✓ Some **speech** (because the passage has plenty, and this gives you an easy way to show how Rat feels).

✓ Think about how the passage shows the Mole's reaction to the river. Take ideas from this and think **how things might be different underground**, from the Rat's point of view.

✓ As always, be as **descriptive** as possible, and use **imaginative language**.

Notice how the example describes the appearance of the brass items in the cupboard, as a way of showing descriptive skill. Also, see how some words are in capital letters, like in the passage. Finally, look at the different ways that speech is presented. This way, it does not become too repetitive.

Marking: In a 5-mark answer, the characters will clearly be the same people as in the passage: they won't have changed their personalities. Their individual traits will be drawn out interestingly. The answer will use most of the answer space, and will include a wide variety of interesting language. It will probably engage with some of the ideas suggested in bullet points above. It will have very few English errors: if there are any, they will be minor. Use your judgement to subtract marks if elements of the above are missing. Marks below 3 (i.e. 1 or 2 marks) should only be awarded if an answer is very weak.   **[5 marks]**

END

Paper 7: *The Picture-Book Giant*

Once there was a fierce, defiant,
Greedy, grumpy, grizzly giant
In the pages of a picture-book, and he
Sometimes screamed, in sudden rages,
5   "I must jump out from these pages,
For this life's a much too humdrum one for me!
Fiddle-dee!
Yes, this life's a quite too quiet one or me!"

So one rainy day he did it,
10 Took the picture-book and hid it,
Stamped his foot, and shouting loudly,
"Now I'm free!"
Boldly started out, forgetting
That he could not stand a wetting!
15 He was just a paper giant, don't you see?
Dearie me!
Just a gaudy, picture giant, don't you see?

    by Evaleen Stein

Blank Page

1.   Choose three adjectives that describe the giant, from lines 1-2. Explain what each one means. You do not need to use full sentences.   **(3)**

....

....

....

2.   Basing your answer on the information in lines 4-6, explain fully why the giant sometimes screams.   **(3)**

....

....

....

....

3.   The giant also shouts in line 11. In your view, what is his reason for doing this?   **(1)**

....

....

....

4.   After the giant has jumped out of the book, he hides it (line 10). Why do you think he does this?   **(2)**

....

....

....

5. Re-write lines 13-14 in your own words. Your answer should show that you understand the ideas in those lines; it does not need to rhyme. Begin like this: "The giant ..." **(4)**

The giant …………..……………………………………………………………………..…..

………………………………………………………………………………………………..

………………………………………………………………………………………………..

6. The poem ends with the words, "don't you see?" What is the poet trying to say? **(2)**

………………………………………………………………………………………………..

………………………………………………………………………………………………..

………………………………………………………………………………………………..

7. Based on lines 3-17, what sort of personality does the giant have? Write down three ideas and give a reason why you believe each one, based on the poem. You do not need to use full sentences. **(6)**

Idea: …………………………………………………………………………………..

Reason: …………………………………………………………………………………..

………………………………………………………………………………………………..

………………………………………………………………………………………………..

Idea: …………………………………………………………………………………..

Reason: …………………………………………………………………………………..

………………………………………………………………………………………………..

………………………………………………………………………………………………..

Idea: …………………………………………………………………………………..

Reason: …………………………………………………………………………………..

………………………………………………………………………………………………..

………………………………………………………………………………………………..

8. What do you imagine the giant is thinking at the end of the story? Make at least two different points, and give a reason for each one. **(4)**

....

....

....

....

....

....

....

TOTAL 25

The Picture-Book Giant – *Solutions*

This text is short, but very peculiar. Working out the plot is tricky; placing yourself in the bizarre position of a picture-book character who decides to escape, but faces problems because he is still made of paper, is more so.

Questions 2 and 7 require strong comprehension skills. 6 and 8 are only possible if you can imagine yourself in the positions of the poet and the giant, respectively.

1.	Choose three adjectives that describe the giant, from lines 1-2. Explain what each one means. You do not need to use full sentences. (3)
Fierce	Angry and maybe scary
Grumpy	Always a bit cross
Defiant	Doesn't like to do what he is told to

Also possible are:

Greedy	Likes to eat more than he needs to
Grizzly	Grey-haired / Cries and complains a lot

This question will look difficult to anybody who has forgotten what an **adjective** is, but in fact **all the describing words in lines 1-2 are adjectives**: if you have a go with confidence, you are likely to do well.

If an explanation is not completely correct, the marker will have to decide whether it is close enough. In some circumstances, a half mark might be given.

Be careful to choose **the easiest three adjectives**. If you are not sure about "grizzly" and "defiant", for example, don't pick these ones!

Marking: 1 mark for each clear explanation of an adjective. 0 marks for an adjective without an explanation. 0.5 marks for a partly correct explanation. **[3 marks]**

2.	Basing your answer on the information in lines 4-6, explain fully why the giant sometimes screams. (3)
	He gets angry because life stuck in the pages of a book is far too boring for him.

This is one of those questions where you have to find the main ideas in a given section, then explain them all ("fully") clearly.

First **put brackets around lines 4-6** (so you don't get lost); then **underline each of the relevant ideas**.

You need to include the following points to get 3 marks:

- ✓ The giant is cross
- ✓ He lives in the pages of a book
- ✓ He finds this boring ("humdrum")

You do not need to write in your own words, but if you simply copy out large parts of lines 4-6 you will not get the marks, because your answer will not show any *understanding*: you must choose **the most relevant ideas**.

Marking: See discussion. **[3 marks]**

---

3. **The giant also shouts in line 11. In your view, what is his reason for doing this?** **(1)**

He is happy and shouts for joy, because at last he is "free".

You need to convey that he is now free from the book, and that he is celebrating this. One of these points without the other might be given a half mark.

Marking: See discussion. **[1 mark]**

---

4. **After the giant has jumped out of the book, he hides it (line 10). Why do you think he does this?** **(2)**

This is so that nobody can make him go back inside it.

Other answers are possible. For example:

He is hiding it in case he changes his mind and needs to get back into the book.

Any sensible idea, clearly explained, should receive 2 marks.

Marking: See discussion. 1 mark for an answer not clearly explained. **[2 marks]**

---

5. **Re-write lines 13-14 in your own words. Your answer should show that you understand the ideas in those lines; it does not need to rhyme. Begin like this: "The giant …"** **(4)**

The giant started walking confidently, but he had forgotten that he would not survive if he got wet.

You will already be used to the process for writing in your own words:

Boldly <u>started out</u>, <u>forgetting</u>
That he <u>could not stand</u> <u>a wetting</u>!

boldly	confidently
started out	started walking
forgetting	(does not need to change: a common word)
could not stand	could not survive
a wetting	getting wet / being rained on

The giant <u>started walking</u> <u>confidently,</u> <u>but he had forgotten</u> that he <u>would not survive</u> if he <u>got wet</u>.

> First **underline the key ideas.**
> Then **think about how each one might best be expressed in English.**
> Finally, **put everything together** in a way that makes sense.

Marking: Full marks if all the key ideas are present, clearly expressed, with consistent use of own words. Subtract marks for missing parts of this.   **[4 marks]**

---

6.   The poem ends with the words, "don't you see?" What is the poet trying to say?   (2)

This is quite a vague question. That's the point: it is testing your ability to come up with an idea!

Broadly speaking, there are **two possible approaches** to answering it, either of which would be correct.

The first option is to **explain what the poet wants us to notice about the giant**:

Although the giant thought that he was free, the poet wants us to understand that he was still the same as ever: a "gaudy" piece of paper that wouldn't survive in the real world.

The other possibility is to **say something about the poem's message**:

The poet wants us to realise that we can't stop being who we are. If we aren't honest with ourselves (like the giant who behaves as though he isn't paper), things might not turn out well.

Any sensible attempt, which includes some effort to explain, should get the marks here.

Marking: 2 marks for a sensible idea, clearly explained. 1 mark if the explanation is incomplete or unclear. **[2 marks]**

---

7. **Based on lines 3-17, what sort of personality does the giant have? Write down three ideas and give a reason why you believe each one, based on the poem. You do not need to use full sentences.** (6)

Idea: He changes mood quickly.
Reason: He has "sudden rages".

Idea: He doesn't think things through.
Reason: He chooses a "rainy day" to leave his book, which is silly because he is made of paper.

Idea: He is very self-confident.
Reason: He sets off "boldly".

The steps for a personality question are as follows:

✓ Find several things that the character does or says
✓ Note (in the margin) what each one says about him
✓ Choose the best and most different three ideas to explain.

Always be careful to **focus on personality/character**.

- Don't write things such as "He is very tall".

Also, make sure that you are talking about **lasting** character traits (the way somebody **usually** is), such as "he is self-confident". Don't write about temporary things, such as "he is annoyed", which might come and go in five minutes.

Marking: 1 mark per good idea that is obviously about personality. 1 mark per clear reason that makes sense. Don't give marks to an idea that is very similar to one already given. **[6 marks]**

---

8.   **What do you imagine the giant is thinking at the end of the story? Make at least two different points, and give a reason for each one.**   **(4)**

I should think he is scared, because he must get back to his "picture-book" before he is soaked and ruined. He might also be feeling embarrassed, because he "started out" so "boldly", but in fact he has been beaten by a bit of rain, even though he is a "fierce" giant.

The question asks what the giant might be "thinking". This **could include feelings**, so long as you give an idea of **what thoughts they might have come from**.

- For example, "embarrassment" is a **feeling**, but based on a sequence of **thoughts**.

Don't get stuck looking for evidence of what the giant *is* thinking. The question asks you to "imagine", so you must put yourself in the giant's position and consider what *you* would feel in those circumstances.

Marking: 1 mark per sensible idea, 1 mark for a supporting reason for each thought.

[4 marks]

END

Paper 8: *"Tiger! Tiger!"*

The boy Mowgli and the wolf Akela have rounded up a herd of buffaloes (led by Rama the bull), with which they will kill Shere Khan, a tiger who is resting in a nearby ravine (valley). They will take the male buffaloes round the outside of the ravine, then send them charging down towards the females at the other end, trapping Shere Khan in between.

Mowgli's plan was simple enough. All he wanted to do was to make a big circle uphill and get at the head of the ravine, and then take the bulls down it and catch Shere Khan between the bulls and the cows; for he knew that after a meal and a full drink Shere Khan would not be in any condition to fight or to clamber up the sides of the ravine.
5   He was soothing the buffaloes now by voice, and Akela had dropped far to the rear, only whimpering once or twice to hurry the rear-guard. It was a long, long circle, for they did not wish to get too near the ravine and give Shere Khan warning. At last Mowgli rounded up the bewildered herd at the head of the ravine on a grassy patch that sloped steeply down to the ravine itself. From that height you could see across
10 the tops of the trees down to the plain below; but what Mowgli looked at was the sides of the ravine, and he saw with a great deal of satisfaction that they ran nearly straight up and down, while the vines and creepers that hung over them would give no foothold to a tiger who wanted to get out.

"Let them breathe, Akela," he said, holding up his hand. "They have not winded him
15 yet. Let them breathe. I must tell Shere Khan who comes. We have him in the trap."

He put his hands to his mouth and shouted down the ravine—it was almost like shouting down a tunnel—and the echoes jumped from rock to rock.

After a long time there came back the drawling, sleepy snarl of a full-fed tiger just wakened.

20 "Who calls?" said Shere Khan, and a splendid peacock fluttered up out of the ravine screeching.

"I, Mowgli. Cattle thief, it is time to come to the Council Rock! Down—hurry them down, Akela! Down, Rama, down!"

The herd paused for an instant at the edge of the slope, but Akela gave tongue in the
25 full hunting-yell, and they pitched over one after the other, just as steamers shoot rapids, the sand and stones spurting up round them. Once started, there was no chance of stopping, and before they were fairly in the bed of the ravine Rama scented Shere Khan and bellowed.

"Ha! Ha!" said Mowgli, on his back. "Now thou knowest!" and the torrent of black
30 horns, foaming muzzles, and staring eyes whirled down the ravine just as boulders

go down in floodtime; the weaker buffaloes being shouldered out to the sides of the ravine where they tore through the creepers. They knew what the business was before them—the terrible charge of the buffalo herd against which no tiger can hope to stand. Shere Khan heard the thunder of their hoofs, picked himself up, and lumbered down

35 the ravine, looking from side to side for some way of escape, but the walls of the ravine were straight and he had to hold on, heavy with his dinner and his drink, willing to do anything rather than fight. The herd splashed through the pool he had just left, bellowing till the narrow cut rang. Mowgli heard an answering bellow from the foot of the ravine, saw Shere Khan turn (the tiger knew if the worst came to the worst it

40 was better to meet the bulls than the cows with their calves), and then Rama tripped, stumbled, and went on again over something soft, and, with the bulls at his heels, crashed full into the other herd, while the weaker buffaloes were lifted clean off their feet by the shock of the meeting. That charge carried both herds out into the plain, goring and stamping and snorting. Mowgli watched his time, and slipped off Rama's

45 neck, laying about him right and left with his stick.

"Quick, Akela! Break them up. Scatter them, or they will be fighting one another. Drive them away, Akela. Hai, Rama! Hai, hai, hai! my children. Softly now, softly! It is all over."

50 Akela and Gray Brother ran to and fro nipping the buffaloes' legs, and though the herd wheeled once to charge up the ravine again, Mowgli managed to turn Rama, and the others followed him to the wallows.

55 Shere Khan needed no more trampling. He was dead, and the kites were coming for him already.

"Brothers, that was a dog's death," said Mowgli.

Adapted from *The Jungle Book*, by Rudyard Kipling

1.   What does the word "lumbered" mean (line 34)?   (1)

    ....

2.   Why can't Shere Khan escape from the buffaloes by climbing out of the ravine?
      Base your answer on lines 1-13.   (2)

    ....

    ....

    ....

3.   Why do Mowgli and Akela choose a "long, long" route (line 6)?   (1)

    ....

    ....

    ....

4.   How does the writer make the buffalo charge exciting in lines 24 to 45? Make
      at least two different points, and give an example from the passage to support
      each one.   (4)

    ....

    ....

    ....

    ....

    ....

    ....

5.   What adjective describes the peacock in line 20?   .... (1)

6.   Write down an adverb from lines 9 or 49.   .... (1)

7.   Write down a noun from line 1.   .... (1)

8.   Write down a verb from the passage, in the:

   (a) past tense   ....

   (b) present tense   ....

   (c) future tense   ....   **(3)**

9.   "As steamers shoot rapids, the sand and stones spurting up round them" (lines
   25 to 26) uses *alliteration*: a repeated consonant sound, "s" in this case. Write a
   sentence of your own that uses alliteration.   **(2)**

....

....

....

10. What do we learn about Mowgli from the passage? Make at least three points,
   and give a reason for each one.   **(6)**

....

....

....

....

....

....

....

....

11.   What does Mowgli mean in the last line, and what do you think makes him want to say this?   **(3)**

....

....

....

....

....

....

TOTAL 25

"Tiger! Tiger!" – *Solutions*

This paper requires a good understanding of parts of speech, and some ability to deal with concepts such as alliteration. However, its main challenge lies in long questions such as 4 and 10.

---

1. **What does the word "lumbered" mean (line 34)?**	**(1)**

It means that Shere Khan walked (or ran) heavily and clumsily.

The word is a bit tricky, but this is only a 1-mark question. If you can work out that it is something to do with Shere Khan walking or running, that should be enough (as long as you aren't directly wrong, for instance saying that he runs lightly or easily), but it is better to give a full explanation – such as in the example.

Marking: See discussion.	**[1 mark]**

---

2. **Why can't Shere Khan escape from the buffaloes by climbing out of the ravine?**	
Base your answer on lines 1-13.	**(2)**

This is because he will be too tired and heavy after "a meal and a full drink".

Or

This is because the sides of the ravine are "nearly straight up and down", so too steep for him to climb.

To get 2 marks, you should explain a point fully. For example, if you say that he is too tired, you should explain that this is because he has been eating and drinking.

Alternatively, **you could briefly make both points** from the example answers above.

Indeed, with a question like this, it is *safest* to make both points, if you can see them, and also give a little explanation.

Notice that **you don't need to repeat the question** ("Shere Khan can't escape from the buffaloes because …"). This would use up a lot of the answer box. People who copy the question often think that they have done enough because they have written a lot of words – but in fact their actual answer, the part that matters, is very short and has not been explained. A phrase like "This is because …" is more useful.

Marking: 1 mark per point, 1 mark per explanation. **[2 marks]**

---

3.   **Why do Mowgli and Akela choose a "long, long" route (line 6)?**   **(1)**

This is so that Shere Khan will not hear them (get "warning").

The example uses **a short quotation** to back up the point. This is always a good idea (unless the question asks for your "own words"), although in this case it is not essential.

People get this question wrong by not explaining why the boy and the wolf have chosen a *long* route. For example, here is an answer that would *not* get a mark:

They choose a "long, long" route so that they can take the male buffaloes to the top and send them charging down onto Shere Khan, who is resting in the ravine.

Nothing about this answer is incorrect, but it doesn't answer the question: Why would they not choose to take the buffaloes by the shortest route possible?

- When you are talking about several animals, you can say "buffaloes" or "buffalo". The text uses "buffaloes".

Marking: See the example above. Any answer expressing the same idea.   **[1 mark]**

---

4.   **How does the writer make the buffalo charge exciting in lines 24 to 45? Make at least two different points, and give an example from the passage to support each one.**   **(4)**

The charge seems unstoppable and overwhelming, because the bulls are compared to a "torrent", "foaming" like "boulders" in a flood. Also, the animals are extremely loud: their "bellowing" makes the valley "ring", and you can imagine being terrified by the sound.

Two points with evidence for each would be enough for 4 marks. Because there is a mark for each point, and a mark for giving evidence to back it up, you could also make four points without evidence, or three points with one piece of evidence. However, it is always wise to do exactly what the question asks, which in this case means giving evidence for each point!

You need to make sure that every point you make focuses on **why the charge is** *exciting* **for the reader** (you). In the example, words like "overwhelming" and "terrified" do this job.

Notice how the example **uses several quotations** – these are the best sort of evidence – but **keeps them all very short**. If you use long quotations, you might end up copying but not explaining.

> **Marking:** 1 mark for each relevant point, and 1 mark for a piece of evidence for each.
> **[4 marks]**

> **5.   What adjective describes the peacock in line 20?**   **(1)**
>
> splendid

An **adjective** describes a noun: here, a "splendid" **peacock**.

> **Marking:** Correct answer only.   **[1 mark]**

> **6.   Write down an adverb from lines 9 or 49.**   **(1)**
>
> steeply

Or "softly". Adverbs often end with "-ly".

> **Marking:** Either "steeply" or "softly".   **[1 mark]**

> **7.   Write down a noun from line 1.**   **(1)**
>
> plan **or** circle **or** Mowgli

"Mowgli" is a *proper noun* – a noun that must take a capital letter.

> **Marking:** Any of the above.   **[1 mark]**

8.	Write down a verb from the passage, in the:	
	(a) past tense	(1)

was

| | **(b) present tense** | (1) |

comes

| | **(c) future tense** | (1) |

will be fighting

These are not the only possible answers!

However, it might be difficult to find verbs in the present and future tense, in a passage written in the past tense. The trick is to notice that these will probably be included in **what the characters** *say*.

For **(c)**, "will" by itself would be worth half a mark. The modal verb "will" creates a future tense when used with another verb ("I will eat"), but arguably is not in the future tense *by itself*. A more specific answer is needed for a full mark.

- Compare "I was cold", in which the past tense "was" is the only verb, and "I will be cold", in which the extra verb "be" is needed.

Marking: Any correct answers.   [3 × 1 mark]

9.	"As steamers shoot rapids, the sand and stones spurting up round them" (lines 25 to 26) uses *alliteration*: a repeated consonant sound, "s" in this case.	
	Write a sentence of your own that uses alliteration.	(2)

With a crack of his club, Kevin sent the ball clattering into the clubhouse kitchen.

Alliterative words do not always need to be next to each other – just close enough that most people would notice the sound of the repeated consonant. You can alliterate with **a repeated sound**, even if the spellings are different ("clubhouse kitchen").

If you use a repeated vowel sound ("Aristotle accepted the apple from Ahmed"), you will only get 1 mark: the question explains that **alliteration involves consonants**.

Marking: 2 marks for a correct example. 1 mark if shows some understanding but not fully correct.   [2 marks]

> **10.   What do we learn about Mowgli from the passage? Make at least three points, and give a reason for each one.   (6)**
>
> Mowgli is skilled at communicating with animals, because he soothes the buffaloes "by voice". He enjoys revenge: when Shere Khan is about to die, he cheers ("Ha! Ha!"). He is patient and careful, because he waits "his time" before taking back control of the herd: he doesn't want to mess up.

Three simple points are absolutely fine here, so long as you give **a clear reason why you think each thing**.

However, don't take the risk of saying anything *too* obvious. Answers such as "he is a boy" or "he has legs" are not likely to impress your marker!

The example is quite repetitive ("Mowgli … because … He … because … He … because"). This structure may not be elegant, but it is clear and makes it easy to get the marks.

> **Marking:** 1 mark per point, plus 1 mark for a supporting reason.   **[6 marks]**

> **11.   What does Mowgli mean in the last line, and what do you think makes him want to say this?   (3)**
>
> He means that Shere Khan's death has been rough and humiliating. He is probably happy about this, because he wanted revenge.

You need to answer both parts of the question clearly. A good answer to one of them might get 2 marks.

> **Marking:** See example and explanation. Different points are acceptable as long as they are fairly similar to the example and a reasonable response to the text.   **[3 marks]**

END

ONE MONTHLY FEE
NO PAYMENT CONTRACT

11 Plus Lifeline is the all-round solution for your child's 11+ preparation. It's also perfect for any child who wants an engaging, enjoyable way to reinforce their Key Stage 2 knowledge.

- Challenging, original practice papers to download and print.
- Fully worked example answers for every question, with step-by-step explanations: like expert private tuition.
- Suitable for independent and grammar schools.
- English Comprehension, Maths, Creative & Persuasive Writing, Reasoning (VR & NVR) and bonus material.
- Written and multiple-choice formats.
- Solutions to real past papers from leading schools – with example answers, discussions and full working.
- Individual marking and feedback available for your child's work.
- Cancel at any time.
- Ideal for children in Years 5 & 6.

"I passed the exam, most of which was because of your help! I don't have an actual tutor like most of my friends, but I feel so lucky to have your papers every week. I think you are the best tutor!" - David Tao, 11

WWW.11PLUSLIFELINE.COM